11/13

W9-BVS-777

The Constellation
Taurus
The Story of the Bull

BY ARNOLD RINGSTAD • ILLUSTRATED BY JT MORROW

The Child's World®

Published by The Child's World®
1980 Lookout Drive • Mankato, MN 56003-1705
800-599-READ • www.childsworld.com

Acknowledgments
The Child's World®: Mary Berendes, Publishing Director
Red Line Editorial: Editorial direction and production
The Design Lab: Design

Photographs ©: US Naval Observatory Library, 5; Shutterstock Images,
7, 17; Enka Parmur/Shutterstock Images, 8; NASA/JPL-Caltech/ESA/
CXC/Univ. of Ariz./Univ. of Szeged, 10; NASA/JPL-Caltech, 11;
Martina I. Meyer/Shutterstock Images, 12; DEA/G. DAGLI ORTI/Getty
Images, 13; Igor Golovniov/Shutterstock Images, 15; Manuel Velasco/
iStockphoto, 16; SSPL/Getty Images, 27

Design elements: Alisafoytik/Dreamstime

ISBN: 9781623234836
LCCN: 2013931376

Printed in the United States of America
Mankato, MN
July, 2013
PA02168

ABOUT THE AUTHOR

Arnold Ringstad lives in Minnesota. He loves looking into the night sky with his telescope.

ABOUT THE ILLUSTRATOR

JT Morrow has worked as a freelance illustrator for more than 20 years and has won several awards. He also works in graphic design and animation. Morrow lives just south of San Francisco, California, with his wife and daughter.

Table of Contents

CHAPTER 1

The Constellation Taurus

An enormous bull rampages through the night sky. He charges with his head down and his sharp horns pointing forward. With a little imagination you can see this nighttime scene. One of the brightest stars in the sky makes up the mighty bull's face. Nearby several stars complete the face's outline. Two stars above the face create the bull's horns. This bull's name is Taurus.

▶ Opposite page: *This image of Taurus appeared in a book from the 1600s.*

What Is a Constellation?

Taurus is a constellation, a collection of stars that forms a pattern in the night sky. Many constellations show creatures or people from Greek **mythology**. A set of 48 constellations was established in ancient times. Today, there are 88 recognized constellations.

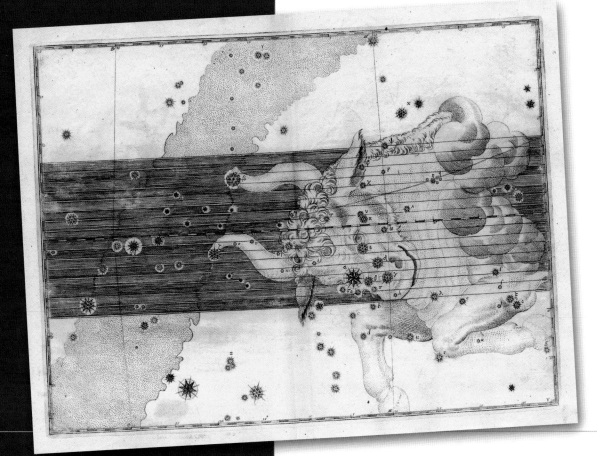

What Is a Star?

Stars are enormous balls of burning gas in space. They are found throughout the **universe**. The closest star to Earth is the Sun. It provides the heat and light that allow life on our planet. The next-closest star is far, far away. Imagine the entire Earth were the size of a grain of sand. Then the nearest star would be more than 6 miles (10 km) away.

If stars are so far away, how can we see so many of them in the night sky? Stars are extremely large. With Earth as big as a grain of sand, the Sun is a ball about 8 inches (.2 m) across. Yet, the Sun is not even the biggest star. Scientists believe the largest stars may be 2,000 times larger than the Sun. If the Sun is an 8-inch (.2 m) ball, the largest stars would be as big as a stadium.

▶ Opposite page: *The Sun is huge compared to the planets in the solar system.*

Sun

Earth

Elnath

Al Hecka

Aldebaran

Hyades

◀ Opposite page: *The stars of Taurus*

Stars in Taurus

The brightest star in Taurus is Aldebaran. It is one of the brightest stars in the entire night sky. It shines with a reddish color. Scientists believe it is 44 times larger than our Sun. Aldebaran is located at one of the bull's eyes.

Near Aldebaran is a group of stars. These stars are packed tightly together. This star cluster is known as the Hyades. With Aldebaran, they form a *V* shape that outlines Taurus's face. Above and to the left of the face are two more stars. These are Elnath and Al Hecka. They make up the tips of the bull's horns. Elnath burns a white color. It is the second-brightest star in Taurus. Al Hecka is a bit dimmer. But it is bright enough to see without a telescope.

Deep-Sky Objects

Objects in space such as star clusters, **nebulae**, and other **galaxies** are known as deep-sky objects. Some are visible with the naked eye, but others require a telescope to see. They are scattered throughout the sky, including within constellations. Two important deep-sky objects in Taurus are the Crab Nebula and the Pleiades.

The Crab Nebula is a huge cloud of gas and dust. It is located near the tip of Taurus's lower horn. Scientists believe that it is left over from a **supernova**, an exploding star. In the year 1054 AD, Chinese astronomers saw the star

▼ This picture of the Crab Nebula shows x-rays in light blue. Visible light is dark blue and green. Heat is shown in red.

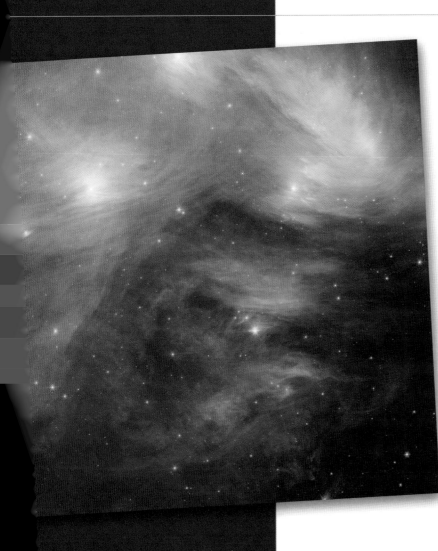

explode. It was so bright that it could be seen during the daytime for nearly a month.

The Pleiades is a star cluster located above and to the right of Taurus's face. It contains large clouds of gas. It also has more than 1,000 stars. However, only six or seven of the stars can be seen without a telescope.

▲ A powerful telescope shows the Pleiades in a cloud of dust. The colors in the image show how hot the dust is. Violet is the coolest and red is the hottest.

CHAPTER 2

The Origin of the Myth of Taurus

The first people to identify the bull in the night sky were the Babylonians of Mesopotamia. They called it the Bull of Heaven. In Babylonian mythology, the hero Gilgamesh had angered the goddess Ishtar. She created the bull to destroy him. Gilgamesh defeated the bull, and the Bull of Heaven was placed in the night sky. The gods were angry with Gilgamesh for killing the bull. They killed his best friend as punishment. Gilgamesh himself was eventually placed in the sky right next to the bull.

THE BABYLONIANS

The Babylonians lived in Babylon, a major city located in modern-day Iraq. The city was created more than 4,000 years ago. The Babylonians developed advanced **astronomy**. They mainly wanted to track the Sun and the moon in order to make more accurate **lunar** and **solar** calendars. The Babylonians also created their own constellations.

▲ The Babylonians decorated the gates leading into their city with bulls and other animals.

The ancient Greeks took many of the Babylonian constellations for themselves. They changed Gilgamesh's constellation to represent their warrior Orion. They also changed the Bull of Heaven into Taurus. In Greek mythology, Orion and Taurus are not connected. Still, the Greeks left them next to each other in the sky.

In Greek mythology, the god Zeus transformed himself into the bull Taurus in order to win the love of the princess Europa. He gave her a ride across the sea. Then he declared his love for her when they reached the island of Crete. She accepted his proposal. She had three sons with Zeus. One was Minos, who became king of Crete.

▶ Opposite page: Zeus the bull rode off into the sea with Europa.

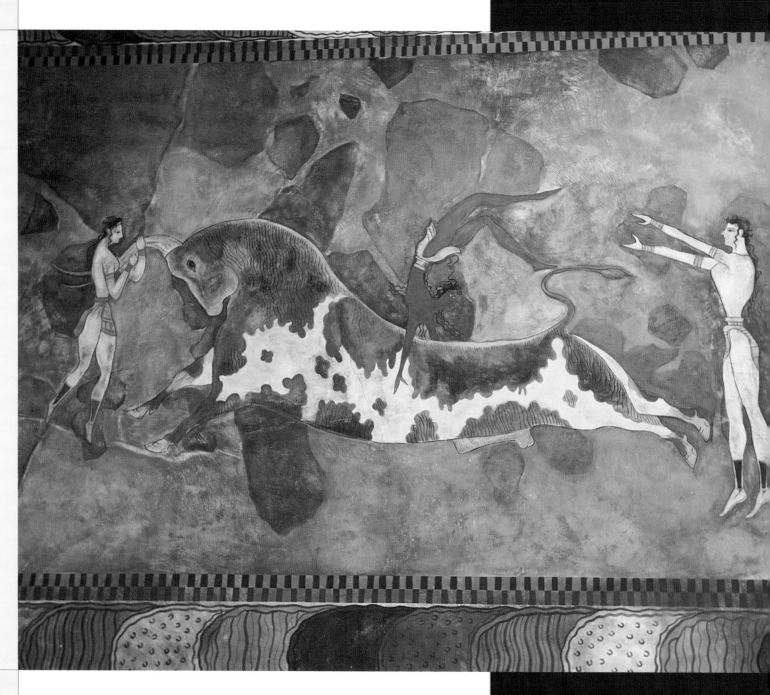

The Greek myth demonstrates how Zeus can achieve anything he wants. He will even transform into an animal if he needs to. It also helps to secure his place as king of the Greek gods. It shows the Greek people that Zeus is incredibly powerful and clever.

The myth also explains why people on the island of Crete worshipped bulls. There are ancient paintings showing bulls in the ruins of the island's palaces. The myth gave the Greek people an explanation for something that existed in their world.

▲ The Greeks worshipped Zeus as the all-powerful king of the gods.

◄ Opposite page: Ancient wall paintings in Crete show bulls in religious scenes.

CHAPTER 3

The Story of Taurus

Long ago, on one of the islands of Greece, there lived a woman named Europa. She was the daughter of King Agenor, who ruled the island. She and her friends were playing near the shoreline one day. Zeus, king of the gods, spotted them. Zeus thought Europa was one of the most beautiful women in the world. He knew right away that he wanted to marry her. But first, he had to think of a plan.

Zeus had many powers. He could hear the thoughts of Europa. He watched her standing near the edge of the water. He heard her wish she could travel away from the island, beyond the horizon.

Suddenly, he knew how to get her to marry him. He called his son, the god Hermes. Zeus told Hermes to drive King Agenor's cattle from their grassy pastures down the hill to the shoreline.

It was time for the next part of Zeus's plan to win Europa's heart. He sneaked into the middle of the herd. Zeus made sure no one was looking. Then he transformed himself into a majestic white bull. Then Hermes began moving the cattle downhill. Zeus stood out clearly among the herd. As he and the other cattle walked down to the water, Europa looked their way.

Most of the cattle walked aimlessly around the beach. But Zeus walked straight toward Europa. As he approached her, she was amazed at the bull's beauty. When he reached Europa, he lowered his head. Europa could tell he wanted her to climb up onto his back. She hesitated at first. But she looked into Zeus's eyes and was reassured. She could tell that the bull loved her. She climbed on. The bull quickly leaped into the sea and began swimming. Europa was alarmed and looked back to the shore. Noticing this, Zeus swam lower in the water. Europa had to hold on even tighter and couldn't look back anymore. Soon, they disappeared over the ocean's horizon.

Europa rode for many hours on the swimming bull's back. Finally, she spotted the island of Crete. They were far away from where they had started. Europa was exhausted from the long journey. The bull was still full of energy, though. He sped up to reach the island even faster.

At last, they reached the beach on Crete. Zeus crouched down to let Europa off his back. She sat down on the sand, completely tired. Suddenly, right before her eyes, the bull transformed into a human form! Zeus immediately began to express his love for Europa. He explained that he was a mighty god. This was how he had turned into a bull. Zeus showered Europa with many gifts. He even gave her a dog that later became the constellation Canis Major. Would she agree to marry him?

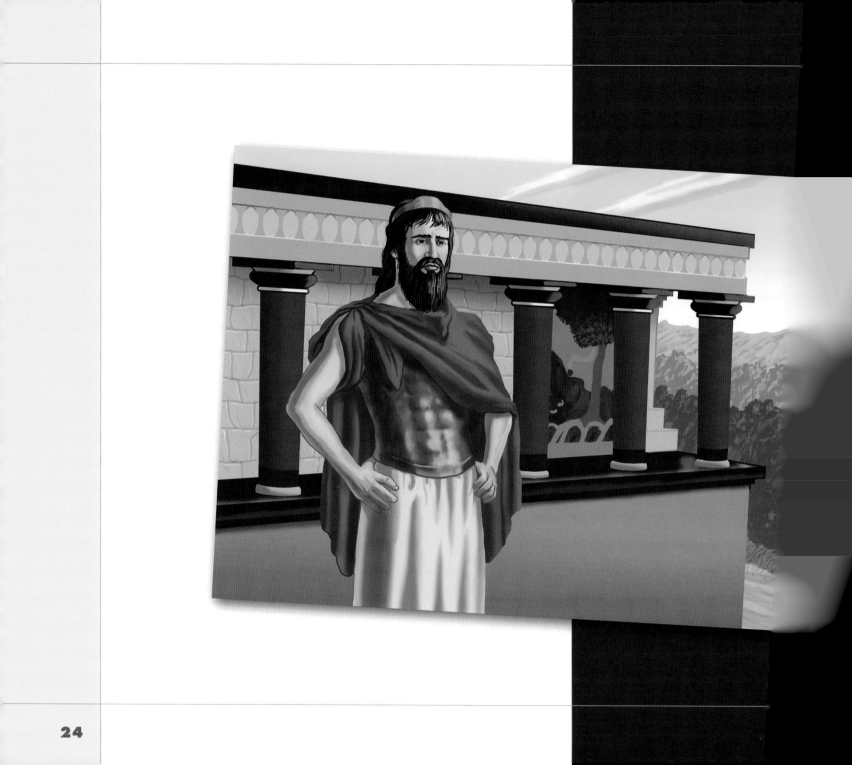

KNOSSOS

The palace of Knossos is an important location for **archaeologists**. It was first uncovered in the year 1900. Since then, archaeologists have found pottery, jewelry, and paintings made thousands of years ago. Subjects of the paintings include dolphins, sporting events, and bulls. These objects have helped us learn more about the daily life of the people who lived in Crete long ago.

Overwhelmed by Zeus's love, Europa agreed to marry him. Zeus and Europa had several children after getting married. Among them was King Minos. Minos later became the ruler of the island of Crete. He established the famous palace of Knossos, known for its bulls.

Zeus later placed the image of the bull into the sky. He wanted to honor his marriage to Europa. It became known as the constellation Taurus. Only the front half of the bull shows in the constellation. This may be because the rest of the bull is underwater, as Zeus swims with Europa.

CHAPTER 4

Taurus in Other Cultures

Chinese astronomers saw different shapes in the sky. They had their own constellations in the area of Taurus. They called the Pleiades Mao and saw it as a hairy head. This is probably because of the hazy appearance of the star cluster.

The other star cluster, called Hyades, was known to the Chinese as Bi. It represented different things to Chinese astronomers. Some saw it as a net used to catch animals. Others saw a group of soldiers led by the bright red star Aldebaran. Between the Pleiades and the Hyades was the Chinese constellation

▶ Opposite page: The bright star Aldebaran and the Pleiades stand for different myths in different cultures.

THE ZODIAC
The night sky is divided into 12 parts. Each part is represented by a constellation. These are called the signs of the **zodiac**. Taurus is one of the 12 signs. The Sun passes through each sign in turn. It takes about a year to go through all 12. The Sun is in Taurus from April 20 to May 20. People born during this time are said to be born under the sign of the bull.

Tianjie. The path between the stars represented the road the emperor took to go hunting.

Most cultures tell stories about the stars in the Pleiades. For example, the Yokut and Monache Native American tribes of California told stories about six sisters. These six sisters left the Earth to become the stars of the Pleiades. Different stories give different reasons why they left. Some say they were too cold or too bored to stay on Earth. In one story, their husbands chased them away because the sisters had eaten too many onions and had bad breath!

CHAPTER 5

How to Find Taurus

The best time to see Taurus is in late autumn. The easiest way to find Taurus is to first find its brightest star, Aldebaran. Look for the bright, reddish star near a small cluster of other stars. It's not far from the three stars in the constellation Orion's belt. Find Aldebaran and the Hyades. Then look above and to the left of them. There you can find Elnath and Al Hecka at the tips of the bull's horns.

Once you've found Taurus, you can find the Pleiades. They will be above and to the right of the bull's face. What else do you see when you look to the stars?

TELESCOPE VIEWING
If you have a telescope, point it toward the Hyades or the Pleiades. It will reveal more stars than you can see with the naked eye. Looking with a telescope lets you see more objects and see them more clearly. An inexpensive telescope can give you good views. It can show nebulae and star clusters, such as the Pleiades and the Hyades. You can even see the rings of Saturn or the ice caps of Mars through a small telescope.

Glossary

archaeologists (ar-kee-AWL-uh-jists)
Archaeologists are scientists who study objects from the past. Archaeologists found artifacts in the ancient ruins.

astronomy (uh-STRAW-nuh-mee)
Astronomy is the study of stars and other objects in space. The Babylonians and the Greeks practiced astronomy.

galaxies (GAL-ax-eez)
Groups of millions or billions of stars form galaxies. Some bright lights in the night sky are galaxies.

lunar (LOO-nur)
Something lunar has to do with the moon. A lunar calendar is based on the moon's movement.

mythology (mith-AH-luh-jee)
Mythology is a culture's set of stories or beliefs. Zeus is a god from Greek mythology.

nebulae (NEB-you-lay)
Nebulae are clouds of gas and dust in space. There are nebulae in the constellation Taurus.

solar (SOHL-ur)
Something solar has to do with the Sun. A solar calendar is based on the Sun's movements.

supernova (soo-per-NOH-vah)
A supernova is a star that explodes suddenly. There was a supernova in Taurus around 1000 AD.

universe (YOU-nih-verse)
The universe is everything that exists in space. The universe is huge and filled with stars.

zodiac (ZOH-dee-ak)
The zodiac is an imaginary circle with 12 wedges that divide the sky. Taurus is a sign of the zodiac.

Learn More

Books

Mitton, Jacqueline. *Zoo in the Sky: A Book of Animal Constellations*. Washington, DC: National Geographic, 2006.

Oberman, Sheldon. *Island of the Minotaur: Greek Myths of Ancient Crete*. Northampton, MA: Crocodile Books, 2003.

Ray, H. A. *Find the Constellations*. New York: Houghton Mifflin, 2008.

Web Sites

Visit our Web site for links about Taurus:

childsworld.com/links

Note to Parents, Teachers, and Librarians:
We routinely verify our Web links to make sure they are safe and active sites.
So encourage your readers to check them out!

Index